# ANDREW LUCK

## BY PAUL HOBLIN

Published by ABDO Publishing Company, PO Box 398166, Minneapolis, MN 55439
Copyright © 2014 by Abdo Consulting Group, Inc. International copyrights reserved in all
countries. No part of this book may be reproduced in any form without written permission
from the publisher. SportsZone™ is a trademark and logo of ABDO Publishing Company.

Printed in the United States of America,
North Mankato, Minnesota
052013
092013

Editor: Chrös McDougall
Series Designer: Craig Hinton

**Photo Credits:** Paul Jasienski/AP Images, cover, 1; Duane Burleson/AP Images, 4; Rick
Osentoski/AP Images, 7; Aaron M. Sprecher/AP Images, 8, 10; Margaret Bowles/AP
Images, 13, 15; Paul Sakuma/AP Images, 16, 20; Marcio Jose Sanchez/AP Images, 19; Icon
Sports Media, 23; Frank Franklin II/AP Images, 24; Phelan M. Ebenhack/AP Images, 27;
Gail Burton/AP Images, 28

Library of Congress Control Number: 2013934745

## Cataloging-in-Publication Data

Hoblin, Paul.
 Andrew Luck: rising NFL star / Paul Hoblin.
   p. cm. -- (Playmakers)
ISBN 978-1-61783-702-9
1. Luck, Andrew, 1989- --Juvenile literature.  2. Football players--United
States--Biography--Juvenile literature.  3. Quarterbacks (Football)--United States--
Biography--Juvenile literature.  I. Title.
796.332092--dc23
[B]                                                            2013934745

# TABLE OF CONTENTS

Andrew Luck

# CHAPTER 1

# ALL-WORLD ATHLETE

 t is common for rookies in the National Football League (NFL) to have up-and-down moments during the season.

The Indianapolis Colts' Week 13 game against the Detroit Lions began as a down moment for rookie quarterback Andrew Luck. He threw three interceptions. With only four minutes left in the fourth quarter, his Colts were losing by 12 points. But with the game on the line, Andrew stopped making

**Andrew Luck scans the field during a game against the Detroit Lions in 2012.**

mistakes and started making plays. He used his quick feet to scramble in and out of the pocket. And he used his strong arm to complete passes. With the clock at 2:47 and ticking, Andrew moved to his left and heaved a perfect 42-yard touchdown strike to wide receiver LaVon Brazill.

The Colts were still down by five points. Andrew and his offense got the ball back with 1:07 on the clock. They needed to go 75 yards with no timeouts left. If they did not score a touchdown, they would lose. Andrew scrambled some more. And he completed more passes. Then the Colts' offense began to struggle. Soon it was fourth down with three seconds left in the game.

Andrew took the snap and hurried to his right. He could not find anyone open in the end zone. So he dumped off the

While Andrew's dad, Oliver Luck, was in the NFL, he took night classes to become a lawyer. He is now the Director of Intercollegiate Athletics at West Virginia University. Andrew's mother, Kathy, also is a lawyer. Andrew is the oldest of four siblings.

Luck looks for a receiver during the Indianapolis Colts' 2012 game against the Detroit Lions.

ball to receiver Donnie Avery. Avery caught the pass, but he was still 10 yards from the end zone. Avery felt as though he was running in slow motion. But he made it. Andrew had thrown two touchdowns in the last three minutes of the game, and the Colts had come from behind to beat the Lions.

NFL fans are often amazed by Andrew's quick feet. But he did not get his quick feet from playing football. He got them from playing soccer.

Luck directs his high school teammates before starting a play during a game in 2006.

Andrew Austen Luck was born September 12, 1989, in Washington DC. However, as a child, Andrew lived in England and Germany. Like most children in Europe, he loved soccer. His favorite team was the Premier League soccer club Arsenal.

Of course, Andrew loved football, too. His dad, Oliver, was an NFL quarterback for several seasons. After he retired from the NFL, Oliver moved his family to Europe and became a general manager in the World League of American Football. A few years later, he was named the league's president. In 2001, Oliver took another sports-related job in Texas. He moved his family back to the United States.

As a sixth grader, Andrew played in a Pop Warner football league. His dad was his coach. During one practice, Andrew began to feel woozy. It turned out he was dehydrated. Summer in Texas is really hot. But that was not the whole story. Andrew had forgotten to drink enough water or eat enough food during the day. His dad was concerned. He sent his son to the bench where he could sit and sip water. But Oliver also was upset with Andrew. He told his son that he needed to be more prepared for practice. His voice was loud enough for Andrew's teammates to hear.

Andrew was really embarrassed. He did not like sitting on the bench when he was not actually injured. He felt as though he had let down his teammates. Ever since, Andrew has been ready to help his team succeed.

Sometimes Oliver Luck would take Andrew to professional soccer games. Andrew enjoyed watching the play on the field, but he also liked looking at the huge stadiums. He still does. When Andrew retires from football, he plans to become an architect so he can design sports stadiums himself.

Andrew Luck

# CHAPTER 2

# STUDENT ATHLETE

Luck went to Stratford High School in Texas. Football in Texas is very competitive. It is rare for a sophomore to start at any position, let alone quarterback. But Luck did just that.

At first, his coaches thought he was really shy. But they soon learned that he had no problem speaking up when he needed to. Toward the end of his first start, Luck's team led 7–6. The only way to guarantee victory was to keep the ball out of the

**Luck gets behind center before taking the snap during a high school game in 2006.**

other team's hands. While in the huddle, Luck shouted words of encouragement to his teammates. Then he guided them on a long drive. Stratford won the game. Luck proved he was more than just talented. He was a leader.

He was also smart. Early in his high school career, Luck's coaches were worried that he would not be able to understand all of the plays. So instead of teaching him the offense, they decided to show him a few plays at a time. But Luck learned so quickly that the coaches quickly changed their minds. It did not take long for him to understand every single play in his team's offense.

In 2006, Luck guided Stratford to the state tournament. In the second round, Stratford played Cypress Falls. Even though Cypress Falls was more talented than Stratford, Luck kept the game close. He threw for four touchdowns and 339 yards. In the

In high school, Luck was so popular that he was almost voted homecoming king—at a rival school. The Stratford quarterback finished third on the homecoming king ballot at Memorial High School.

Luck scrambles away from a defender during a high school game in 2008.

end, Stratford lost by a single point. But Luck showed that he could play well against one of the top teams in the state.

Luck not only starred on the field, he starred in the classroom, too. Luck ended up being Stratford's valedictorian. That meant he had the best grades in his class. In fact, he cared as much about his schoolwork as he did about football. He wanted his teachers to treat him as a student, not an athlete.

That must have been tough to do. Luck might have been a great student, but he was also one of the top high school

Coming out of high school, Luck was ranked the fourth-best quarterback in the nation by Scout.com. That Web site tracks the best high school football players for college fans.

quarterbacks in the nation. By the end of his high school career, Luck had thrown for 7,139 yards and 53 touchdowns. He was recruited to play for most of the top college programs in the country. Among those schools were the University of Alabama, Louisiana State University, and the University of Oregon.

But Luck did not want to go to a school simply because it had a great football team. He wanted to go to a school with great academics, too. So he looked for a school that would challenge both his body and his mind. Eventually he found it.

Andrew Luck was going to Stanford University.

**Luck gets ready to pass for a first down during a 2008 game while at Stratford High School in Texas.**

Andrew Luck

# CHAPTER 3

# STANFORD STANDOUT

**S**tanford is a great academic school, but it did not have a very good football team. Two years before Luck arrived, the Cardinal's record was just 1–11. They were not much better the year after that. They finished the season with only four wins and eight losses.

During Luck's first year at Stanford, his coaches asked him if he would like to start. Luck told them he would rather wait his turn. The quarterback who had

**Luck celebrates after scoring a touchdown for Stanford during a 2009 game.**

been starting was a senior. Luck did not want to take the starting job before he had earned it.

The next year, in 2009, Luck was ready to take over as Stanford's quarterback. He led the team to an 8–5 record and helped the offense score the most points in school history. Stanford also went to its first bowl game since 2001.

In 2010, the team was even better. The Cardinal finished the season with a 12–1 record. They capped their season by beating Virginia Tech 40–12 in the Orange Bowl. It was the Cardinal's first-ever Bowl Championship Series (BCS) bowl game victory. The BCS bowls are the most important.

The main reason for Stanford's success was its quarterback. That season Luck threw for 3,338 yards. And his 32 touchdown passes were the most in school history. He was named his conference's Offensive Player of the Year. He was also a finalist

Luck set Stanford's record for single-season touchdown passes. John Elway had held the previous record. Elway went on to a Hall of Fame career in the NFL after leaving Stanford. He led the Denver Broncos to two Super Bowl victories.

Luck drops back to pass during Stanford's 2010 game against the University of Southern California.

for the Heisman Trophy. It is awarded to the best player in college football each season.

Perhaps the highlight of the season was the Cardinal's 37–35 victory over the University of Southern California. With time running out, the Cardinal found themselves behind 35–34. Earlier in the game, their kicker had missed an extra point. It looked as though that miss was going to be the difference in

**Luck poses in Stanford's trophy room in February 2011.**

the game. But Luck was determined to drive down the field and give his kicker another chance. Luck followed through. He completed three passes. Stanford drove from its own 26-yard line to the opposing 12-yard line. And with four seconds left, Stanford's kicker trotted onto the field and made a 30-yard field goal. Just like that, the kicker had become the hero.

By the end of the season, many people believed that Luck was going to be the first player picked in the NFL Draft. That meant he would be a millionaire by the next fall.

There was only one problem with that theory: Luck was not sure he wanted to leave school yet. For one thing, he had not yet finished his architecture degree. For another, he liked being a student. Luck enjoyed riding his bicycle to class and hanging out with his friends. He liked his teammates. He even liked the lack of attention he got on campus. Luck wanted to be treated as just another college student.

Staying at college was a big risk, though. If Luck got seriously injured, his dreams of playing in the NFL could be shattered. So he had a difficult decision to make. He talked it over with family, coaches, and friends. Then he contacted NFL quarterback Peyton Manning. Manning was Luck's childhood hero. And he had made a similar decision when he was in college. Manning's advice was simple: If you choose to stay in college, promise yourself you will not regret it.

Luck eventually decided to turn down all the money the NFL would bring. He returned to Stanford to finish his degree and play one final season of college football. Some people thought he was crazy. But Luck made the decision with no regrets.

In 2011, Luck broke his own record for touchdown passes in a single season. Once again he was named the Pacific-12 Conference's Offensive Player of the Year.

Luck's team also had another excellent year. The Cardinal won 11 games and only lost two. During a win against the University of Washington, the Cardinal set a single-game school rushing record. They ran for 446 yards. After the game, Stanford's coach tried to apologize to Luck. He thought Luck might have been angry. After all, Luck was vying for the Heisman Trophy. A blowout win would have been a good chance to throw for more yards and touchdowns. Instead, the coach had decided to keep running the ball.

Luck was not mad, though. He was happy. His team had gotten the win, and he had helped out by handing the ball to

In the NFL, the team with the worst record gets the first pick in the next season's NFL Draft. Some football fans wanted Luck on their team so badly that they wanted their team to lose on purpose. A few Indianapolis Colts fans already had Luck jerseys made while he was still a senior at Stanford.

Luck sets up to pass during Stanford's 2011 game against the rival University of California Golden Bears.

his running backs. His coach knew then that Luck cared more about the team than himself. Luck ended up finishing second in the Heisman Trophy voting again that year.

A few months later, the Indianapolis Colts made Luck the first pick of the 2012 NFL Draft. He also graduated Stanford with a degree in architectural design.

*Andrew Luck*

# CHAPTER 4

# RECORD-SETTING ROOKIE

**E**veryone agreed that Luck's future was bright. Assuming he did not get hurt, he had both the talent and the intelligence to become a star in the NFL. What people did not agree on was when this would happen.

After all, playing quarterback as a rookie is never easy. Luck's situation was especially tricky. His new team, the Indianapolis Colts, had won only two games the previous season. And if that was not bad

**NFL commissioner Roger Goodell poses with Luck after the Colts picked Luck in the 2012 draft.**

enough, Luck had to replace the legendary Peyton Manning at quarterback.

Luck's first game did not go well. The Colts lost to the Chicago Bears 42–21. Luck threw three interceptions. But he also tossed his first NFL touchdown. The next week Luck and the Colts faced the Minnesota Vikings. Along with two more touchdown passes, Luck led the Colts on a game-winning drive.

A few weeks later, Colts coach Chuck Pagano was diagnosed with leukemia. The Colts did their best to support their coach during this difficult time. Orange stickers were placed on lockers to raise awareness for the disease. And some players wore orange gloves for the same reason.

When the team saw their coach again, he was bald. His treatment had caused his hair to fall out. In another sign of

In his 13 seasons as the Colts' starter, Peyton Manning was named to 11 Pro Bowls, won four Most Valuable Player Awards, and won a Super Bowl. But Manning had missed the 2011 season due to neck surgery. And the Colts had decided it was time to move on. Manning went to the Denver Broncos, and the Colts drafted Luck.

Luck and his Indianapolis Colts teammates shaved their heads to honor coach Chuck Pagano, who had leukemia.

support, several players shaved their heads. Luck was one of these players. Luck and his teammates were determined to play the season in honor of Pagano. Their efforts became known as "CHUCKSTRONG."

In a Week 5 game against the Green Bay Packers, Luck led the offense on another game-winning drive. With 35 seconds left, Luck completed a pass to wide receiver Reggie Wayne.

Luck looks to pass against the Baltimore Ravens in the playoffs after the 2012 season.

Wayne then twisted and lunged into the end zone for the deciding touchdown.

Three weeks later, Luck played in his first overtime game. His touchdown pass to running back Vick Ballard gave the Colts a 19–13 victory over the Tennessee Titans. The very next week, Luck threw for 433 yards, a new rookie record. The Colts beat the Miami Dolphins, 23–20.

By week 13, Luck had already guided his team on four game-winning drives. But none of them were as impressive as the one he led against the Detroit Lions. That last-second win was the Colts' eighth victory of the season. And they were not done winning. With two more wins the Colts qualified for the playoffs.

The Colts had one regular-season game left. It was against the Houston Texans. This one was special. Pagano was again on the sidelines. His leukemia was in remission. Before the game he thanked his players for all the support they had given him.

Luck celebrated his coach's return by throwing for two more touchdowns. Over the season, he threw for 4,374 yards, a rookie record. More importantly, he had once again turned a losing team into a winning team. His Colts beat the Texans, giving Indianapolis a record of 11–5.

Indianapolis lost in the first round of the playoffs. But it had still been an amazing season. The Colts had won nine more games than the year before. And in Luck, they had found their star of the future.

Luck might have been a star, but he was still treated as a rookie. He had to carry his teammates' jerseys after practice. It is an NFL tradition for rookies to do basic tasks for their older teammates.

# FUN FACTS AND QUOTES

- While at Stanford, Andrew Luck became friends with another famous athlete: professional golfer Michelle Wie.

- Luck's first position in football was not quarterback. It was defensive end.

- Luck's younger sister, Mary Ellen, plays volleyball at Stanford.

- As much as Luck loved being a student, he still loves football even more. "I'd probably go crazy if I couldn't play football," he said.

- Luck loves to read. His favorite genre is historical fiction. His favorite book is *Papillon*.

- Luck's 11 wins in 2012 were the most ever by a rookie who was taken first in the NFL Draft.

## WEB LINKS

To learn more about Andrew Luck, visit ABDO Publishing Company online at **www.abdopublishing.com**. Web sites about Luck are featured on our Book Links page. These links are routinely monitored and updated to provide the most current information available.

# GLOSSARY

**architect**
Someone who designs buildings and structures.

**bowl game**
An extra game winning college football teams play at the end of the season. The games are usually played in late December or January.

**draft**
An annual event in which NFL teams select the top college football players.

**drive**
A sustained movement downfield by the team on offense.

**interceptions**
In football, passes thrown to a teammate but caught by someone on the opposing team.

**leukemia**
Cancer of the blood or bone marrow.

**recruited**
When college coaches try to convince a high school player to join their teams.

**remission**
When cancer responds to treatment and starts to get better.

**rookie**
A first-year player in the NFL.

**scramble**
When a quarterback takes off running with the ball, usually to avoid pressure from the defense.

# INDEX

## FURTHER RESOURCES

Gitlin, Marty. *Peyton Manning*. Edina, MN: ABDO Publishing Co., 2011.

Peloza, Brian. *Indianapolis Colts*. Edina, MN: ABDO Publishing Co., 2010.

Wilner, Barry. *The Super Bowl*. Minneapolis, MN: ABDO Publishing Co., 2013.